BUSINESS RESET 2.0

How To Fix Your Business When The Wheels Fall Off.

Especially When Your Business Grows…

Book One of Four

By Your Business Reset Expert

Peter Maheux

BusinessReset.com

How To Fix Your Business When The Wheels Fall Off.
Especially When Your Business Grows…
Print
ISBN-13: 978-1511858793

ISBN-10: 1511858796

Design by Tom Lilly, T Graphics • www.TGraphics.ca

Edited by Sheryl Bennett-Wilson, Words For Sale

These books are dedicated in loving memory to my wife Jay.

She was my partner in every way.

Without her support and encouragement these books would not exist.

Jay passed away in October of 2012.

I continue to miss her every day.

Welcome to Business Reset 2.0.

I'm Peter Maheux and I really can help you setup Your Business for success, fix it if things are not going well, reset it if you want to expand or diversify – or both. It doesn't matter if you plan to or are already running your own business. If you have a small to medium size business or you are a small to medium size organization within a large business (*yes, all the information in these books has and can be used effectively by organizations and departments within large organizations*) the information in these books will help you be successful at meeting your objectives and goals.

These books – this is Book One in a four part series - will literally help you 'connect the dots' for your business. By following the simple steps involved you'll actually be able to 'see' how your business operates and fully understand where the problem is and how to fix it 'when the wheels fall off'. Your business will be transformed back into the highly functioning entity that you wrote about in your business plan/objectives and dreamed of.

No expensive consultants. No computer programs to buy. I will walk you through the process of literally '*being your own consultant*'. You'll end up with a Big Picture of your business, forms, procedures and documents that are relevant specifically to your business and a blueprint you can refer to so that you can always reset and '*fix your business when the wheels fall off*'.

Here's an example of where I'm coming from. A few years ago I was doing lectures across North America on a process called DFMA – Design For Manufacture and Assembly. I decided to try an experiment at one of my workshops. I gave the same product assembly to two different product design groups. The first group was told to use the DFMA software analysis tools to come up with a more cost effective design solution. The second group was told to analyze the product using the fact gathering spreadsheets I'd designed for the exercise. The second group had to gather facts, think through the cost reduction process and fully understand the total use of the product. The results were astonishing. Group one reduced the product by 47%. But they didn't know whether their solution would meet all required application needs. Group two had reduced the product by a staggering 88%. Not only that, they had a clear understanding of the total application of the product. I realized that people make the difference, not the tools and that *all* the design impacting information had to be developed *before* any actual product development could begin.

By following the steps outlined in each one of the Business Reset books, your business will be designed for effectiveness, you'll have excellent communication processes, your employees will understand and know their roles, responsibilities and rewards, you'll always hire the right people, your business will be successful and you'll have peace of mind and a balanced lifestyle. You'll also know exactly when one of your 'wheels' is loose and what to do about it.

Let's fix your business…

Is this Your Business?

You've launched a new business. Your expectations are high. Your operations are simple and easy to manage. Your hours are reasonable. Life is good.

Your business grows - substantially. You start to experience small operational problems. You're not sure how to address them. You let them go. Your business continues to grow. Your operational problems grow too. You start to lose revenue. Your hours become unreasonable. Your family life suffers. You may lose your business.

What the heck happened?

Your Business changed. As a Business Reset expert I've seen it all before. Your Businesses success is actually getting in the way of how you manage on a day-to-day basis. You need to step back and list what has changed. I can help you reconnect the dots with solutions that are long term and permanent. You won't need new software. There are no huge consulting fees.

Using this book as a guide, your business will undergo a transformation. Together we'll accomplish a Business Reset. I'll help you get back to the basics of what made Your Business successful in the first place.

Let's get started!

Peter Maheux

Business Reset Expert

Table of Contents

CHAPTER ONE

How Your Business Was Born, Grew And Expanded.

How Your Business was Born

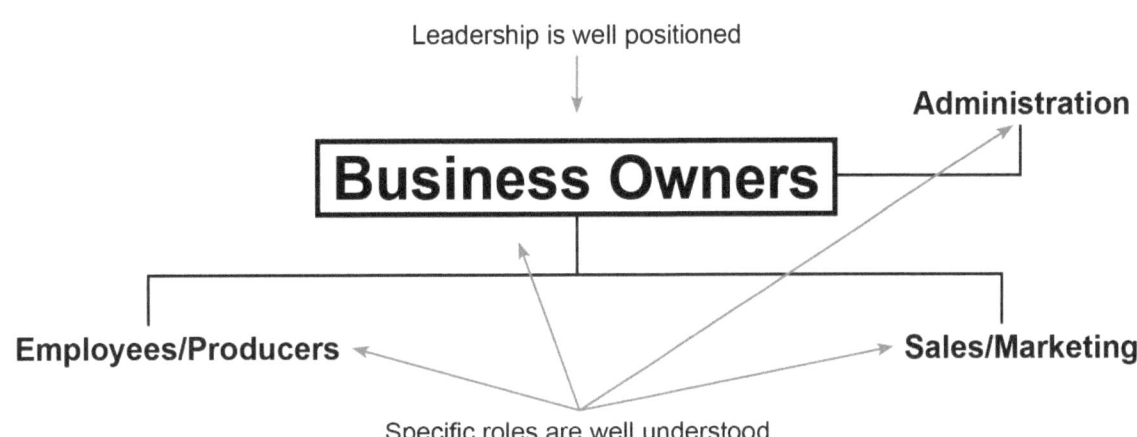

You developed a business case. You included short and long term goals and expected revenue growth for a two to five year period. You also included your staffing and facility needs. Your plan was approved. You hired your staff, started producing, built your customer list, promoted your products and/or services and started building your cash flow.

At the beginning, Your Business was small. You understood your role and so did your staff. Any problems or issues were discussed and resolved quickly and efficiently. You and your staff don't have a lot to manage except basic business activities.

Typical Operating Dynamics of a New Business

Your Businesses volumes are easily managed. Your employees may even be located within eyesight and talking distance. Your Business has a team mindset. You all have excellent supportive attitudes towards each other and Your Businesses goals.

You are on top of everything and critical decisions are easily made. Your employees feel good and have a high degree of trust. You have adequate time to do a good job, take a coffee break and hold informal discussions with your employees.

You and your employees have controlled stress levels, balanced lives and time for family and socializing.

Your Business is good.

Life is good.

What could possibly go wrong?

Then Your Business Grew

- Your cash flow increased substantially.

- Your hours of work doubled.

- Your operational processes are having difficulty handling the increased business.

- Your customer demand is high.

- You added more employees.

- Quality and safety are now issues.

Your Business is still successful, the money is coming in. But there are signs of work overload and stress slowly creeping into the day-to-day functioning of Your Business. Some tasks are becoming overwhelming.

Your Businesses success is getting in the way of how you manage on a day-to-day basis.

- Your work hours and your employee's work hours start to increase to keep up the demand.

- You start going to the office on weekends. You don't have time during the week anymore to go over the books and make sure Your Business is financially on track.

- You begin to spend more and more time on employee questions which takes time away from your focus on the market and customer base.

- Your employees complain about your slow computers because the files and information they have to process has grown.

- Your office supply inventory runs out. This has never happened before.

- You and your partner and your employees notice occasional bouts of negative stress.

- You and your employees have to produce more in the same time period.

- Your setup must produce more in the same time period.

BUT

Instead of stepping back and taking the time to figure out what's going on, you expanded.

You Expand Your Business

Your Business hires more employees. You need them to keep up with demand and to allow you to focus on your customer base and the market. You re-invest some of your earnings to expand. You need to cover your computer networks, your tools, your inventory, office supplies, filing systems and production equipment.

You expand your square footage. You identify the new skills needed for the business. You get ready to purchase the required equipment.

NOW

Do any of these apply to Your Business?

- Your Business can't keep up with product demand.

- Your customers can't reach you and messages go missing.

- Your files are a mess and key information is missing.

- Your books are a mess – you can't tell if you are making or losing money.

- Your employees have conflicts, are absent, deliver a poor performance or leave.

- Your inventory is impossible to keep track of.

- Your deliveries were late and you've lost clients over quality or service.

- Your computer systems are failing.

- Your business has become your life and you're completely stressed out.

If you're nodding your head in agreement with even three of the above issues, you need to step back and list what has changed - it's the first step to a Business Reset and putting the wheels back on.

WARNING

TWO TRAPS TO AVOID WHEN YOU MAKE CHOICES FOR YOUR BUSINESS

TRAP #1 – PURCHASING SOFTWARE TOOLS

You look at excellent software that can track inventory, organize and retrieve files and prioritize and schedule all your production work. It sounds like a problem solver.

HOWEVER:

You need to know that YOU will have to populate all the databases in the software before the software tool becomes of any use to you.

Your new software tool may lie dormant in your computer and never be fully implemented.

TRAP SOLUTION:

Use basic spreadsheet tools.

You'll find basic spreadsheets simple and easy to implement. You'll still need someone to input your information but it's a less expensive solution. Make sure you keep a history of how it's done so someone else can do it.

TRAP #2 – HIRING NEW EMPLOYEES

Your hiring of new employees will be one of the biggest investments Your Business will make. Get it right the first time. Hiring the wrong person can destroy business morale and trust.

TRAP SOLUTION:

Your Business can benefit - *'Book Four – Hire the Right Person - Always…'*

Avoid overlaps in responsibilities with other employees. Your Business procedures and training have to be done up front. Your loyal, existing employees need to be participants in the hiring process.

Congratulations!

You've taken the first steps in transforming Your Business. You've probably already got an idea of 'where the wheels feel like they're falling off'. Let's keep going for the 'why' and 'how' to fix it.

Now, do a Chapter Checklist – it'll help you remember some of the things you've discovered about Your Business.

CHAPTER CHECKLIST:

Do a simple diagram of how Your Business works. For example, sales brings in an order, use an arrow to indicate where it goes next, then keep going through to the end product or service. You'll find some useful symbols in Chapter Five. Use the space below and sketch it in.

List below what worked really well when you started Your Business.

_____
_____
_____
_____
_____
_____
_____

List some of the issues you started to have as Your Business started to grow.

_____
_____
_____
_____
_____
_____
_____

List issues you started to face as you expanded – try to be as specific as possible.

_____

_____

_____

_____

_____

_____

_____

What are your potential traps?

_____

_____

As you've written things down you're probably getting a better idea of just some of the issues Your Business is facing. In Chapter Two I'll show you why Your Business needs a transformation with a Business Reset.

Make notes below of other issues Your Business is facing:

CHAPTER TWO

Why Your Business Wheels Are Falling Off

So everything was going hunky-dory with Your Business. You got really successful. You expanded. You hired more staff. You moved to a larger facility and bought more equipment.

BUT

Your Business is experiencing rapid growth.

To manage this growth, you have put in place employee roles and responsibilities – to ensure that everything to be done was covered. You also put in place processes and procedures – to deal with product quality and operational safety. You and your employees had to develop these documents to ensure things are done correctly and repeatedly done correctly.

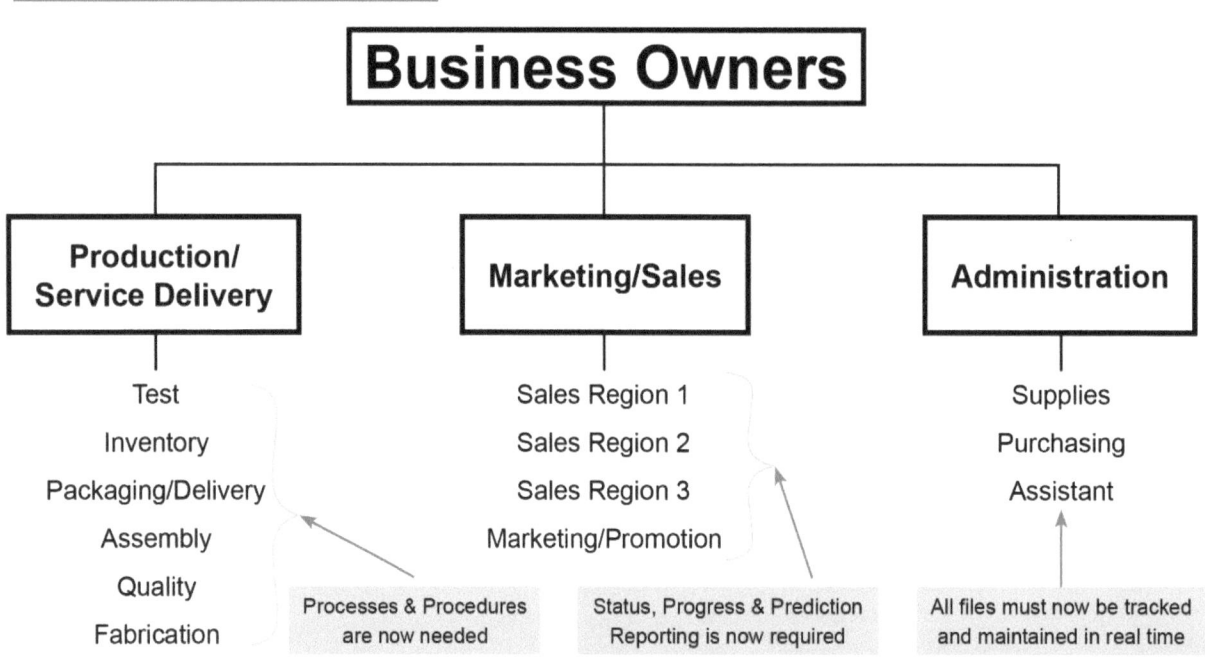

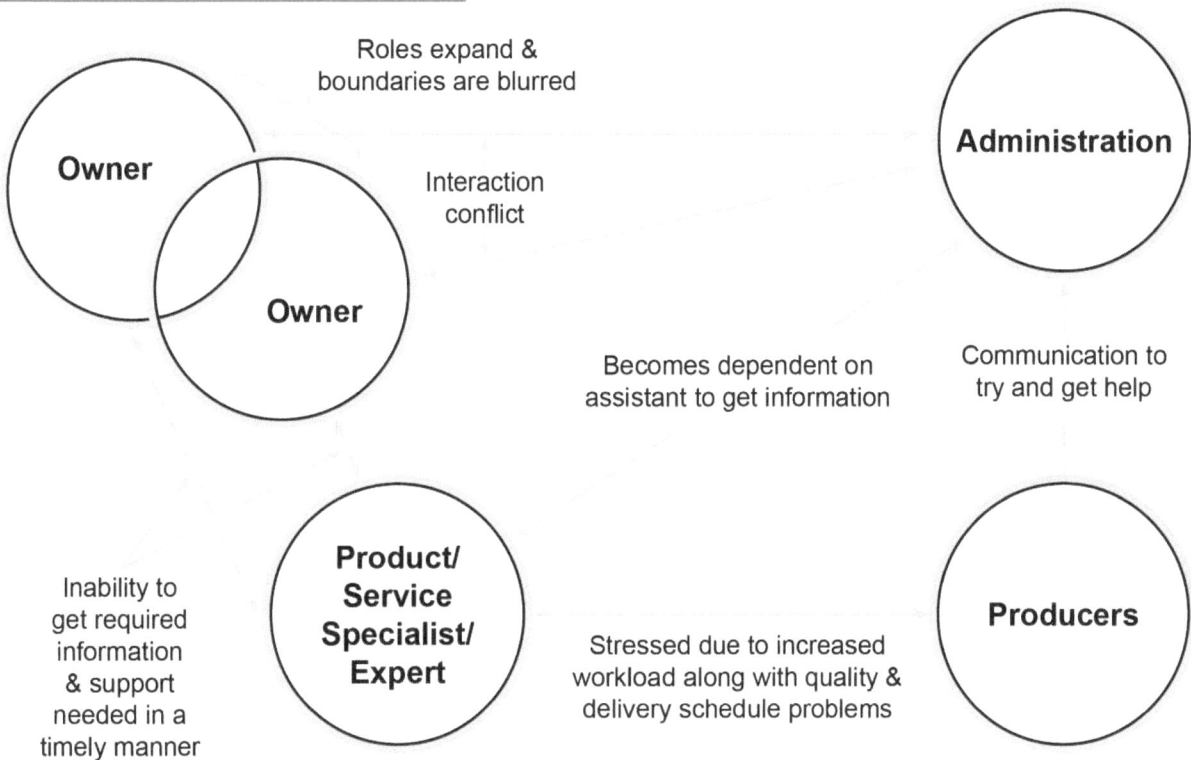

The Dynamics of What Happens When Business Growth is not Managed

Roles expand & boundaries are blurred

Owner

Interaction conflict

Owner

Administration

Becomes dependent on assistant to get information

Communication to try and get help

Inability to get required information & support needed in a timely manner

Product/ Service Specialist/ Expert

Stressed due to increased workload along with quality & delivery schedule problems

Producers

Do any of these apply to Your Business?

- Your diminished lines of communication result in confusion.

- You or your employees are duplicating work.

- Your work hours have increased.

- Your stress levels have increased on the job and at home.

- Your overall efficiency has decreased dramatically.

- Your workplace isn't enjoyable anymore.

- Your employees become 'clock-watchers'.

YOUR BUSINESS IS SUFFERING FROM UNMANAGED GROWTH

Symptoms of Unmanaged Growth

Dynamics	Symptoms
A. Business Owners Roles Expand	1. Stress level increases 2. Hours of work increase 3. Life balance is impacted 4. Blame happens 5. Required marketing actions slip 6. Sales follow-up activities decrease 7. Owners can no longer back each other up
B. Owners Pushing Administration Harder	8. Phone Messages get misplaced 9. Administration is no longer sure who is the boss 10. Files go missing 11. Administration is not sure who was talking to whom
C. Product Specialist Needs Timely Decisions More Frequently	12. Problems not addressed when they need to be 13. Reduced trust of owners 14. Performance level drops
D. Producer Pressuring Administration More Often	15. Employee conflict 16. Administration's ability to get work done is impacted 17. Confidential files are seen
E. Product Specialist More Dependent on Administrations for Decisions	18. Trust level of owners impacted 19. Administration overworked 20. Files get misplaced 21. Office supplies/equipment are lacking
F. Increased Workload for All Employees	22. Delivery schedule is difficult to manage & keep up to date 23. Product quality issues occur 24. There are safety issues 25. Employee dissatisfaction expressed 26. Absenteeism exists 27. Employees leave

Your Business focus has shifted to producing documents and maintaining documents. Your product or service suffers. ALL your employees are likely not familiar with the processes or procedures because you've not had time to train them. Your Business is becoming more and more difficult to manage.

Congratulations!

I mean it. You're serious about fixing Your Business and finding out why the wheels are coming off. Go through the Chapter Checklist below. It will help you start to frame a picture of Your Business.

CHAPTER CHECKLIST:

Do another simple diagram of how Your Business works.

Put a check mark beside the symptoms below that apply to Your Business.

Increased stress ___ Increased work ___ Home/work balance affected ___
Employees placing blame___ Required marketing slips ___ Sales follow-ups decrease ___
No back up between owners ___ Phone messages lost ___ Admin not sure who to report to ___
Files go missing ___ Admin not sure which departments talking to each other ___
Problems not addressed ___ Reduced trust of owners ___ Performance drops off ___
Employee conflict ___ Admin not getting work done ___ Confidential files viewed ___
Supplies/equipment lacking ___ Delivery schedule becomes unmanageable ___
Product quality issues ___ Safety issues ___ Employees expressing dissatisfaction ___
Absenteeism increases ___ Employees quit ___

List the procedures and processes you've put in place to deal with some of the above issues.

_____

_____

_____

_____

_____

_____

_____

_____

_____

_____

Write down the issues that you resolved, the ones that remain and why you think any outstanding issues are still unresolved.

_____

_____

_____

_____

_____

_____

_____

_____

You've probably got a good idea now about 'why' the wheels seem to be falling off. The difficult task in Your Business transformation is often connecting the dots. In Chapter Three I'll explain 'how' a Business Reset works. I'll also provide an example of how a company's production line found an easy solution to an issue that was costing them millions.

CHAPTER THREE

How The Business Reset Process Will Put The Wheels Back On

You've likely realized by now that things have changed in Your Business. The next step is how to transform Your Business with *long-term permanent solutions*. No 'quick-fix' software solutions, no expensive coaching sessions. The key to you discovering 'how' to transform Your Business is contained in the Business Reset 12 Step Process in Chapter Four.

Right now, using your notes from Chapters One and Two, step back and make a list of what's changed in Your Business.

_____

_____

_____

_____

_____

_____

_____

_____

_____

_____

_____

Doing a BUSINESS "RESET" will:

- Allow you to regain control and effectively manage your day-to-day operations.

- Provide reasonable hours for you and your employees.

- Meet and/or exceed customer expectations.

- Ensure goals and objectives are translating into financial profit.

- Result in financial success and a healthy balanced lifestyle for you, your family and your employees.

You will be able to identify:

- Your Business roadblocks.

- Your operational problems.

- Your critical processes.

- You and your employees will have a better understanding of Your Business.

Your Business will be back in business.

How an easy solution helped save a company millions.

Yes, millions. This was one of those situations where you're quite literally left shaking your head. The company was bleeding money – hundreds of thousands every day. Their production was down, they had contracts to fill but they couldn't get anything off the assembly-line. Senior management was blowing a gasket. Mid-management was holding meeting after meeting to try and resolve the problem and Sales was placating customers left and right – 'We'll have it by next week'. But even though all the component parts were flowing nicely down the line, by the time they got to the end production just seemed to halt.

Because of my expertise and my ability to pinpoint exactly where the problem might be, I was asked to a meeting of senior management to try and figure it out. They explained their problem, what they thought the issues were and offered to walk me through the production process. Instead, I told them I'd like to walk the production line by myself. I didn't want to prejudge and I wanted to get my own assessment of the situation.

To quote Johnny Cash, 'I walked the line'. They had a great assembly line. All the procedures and processes were being followed – flawlessly. But when I finally got to the last small procedure on the line, things fell apart. The final part of the production procedure was to secure a lock on the outer metal cabinet. The lock was actually a marvel of engineering but needed a delicate touch to screw it into place. The production-line worker was using a standard Phillips screw driver. Every time he turned the screw he ruined it. Instead of saying something or using another type of screw driver, he was pulling the works out of the cabinet and tossing the entire unit. He would then put the component parts into another cabinet, try to tighten the lock and ruin it again. No wonder the company's production was down to less than 18% a day. No one from management or a senior line supervisor had ever tried to determine why there were so few units being produced and ready to ship.

I asked the worker if a different type of screw driver would work, like a plastic one. He indicated that would likely solve the problem. So we made a quick visit to their machine shop and had one of the machinists create a plastic screw driver to his specifications. We went back to his station on the production line. The plastic screw driver worked perfectly and within minutes he was able to put the finishing turns on several units. I returned to the board room and explained that the problem was solved.

Sure enough, by the next day the assembly line was up to almost full capacity and the units were being shipped out the door as soon as they came off the last part of the assembly line.

SO WHAT'S THE POINT?

The point is that without me going step-by-step through their production process the problem would never have been solved. Management would have continued to point fingers at the line supervisors, the line supervisors would have pointed fingers at all the workers and still be baffled as to the problem. Sales would have still been hollering at everyone.

Yes, this was for a large company with an assembly line BUT even if you're a small 'Mom and Pop' snack bar you'll be able to pinpoint where the problem is when the sandwich orders get backed up.

If you want to find out 'where the wheels are falling off' you have to do a Business Reset.

Congratulations!

You've made a commitment to find out why Your Business is stalled with a Business Reset. Yes it's going to take you some time, but once you're done you'll have transformed Your Business and have ***long-term permanent solutions*** and isn't Your Business worth it?

Chapter Four contains The Business Reset 12 Step Process. Don't worry. I'll make sure we go through it in non-intimidating chunks of three steps at a time with plenty of check lists to help.

CHAPTER FOUR

The Business Reset Twelve Step Process

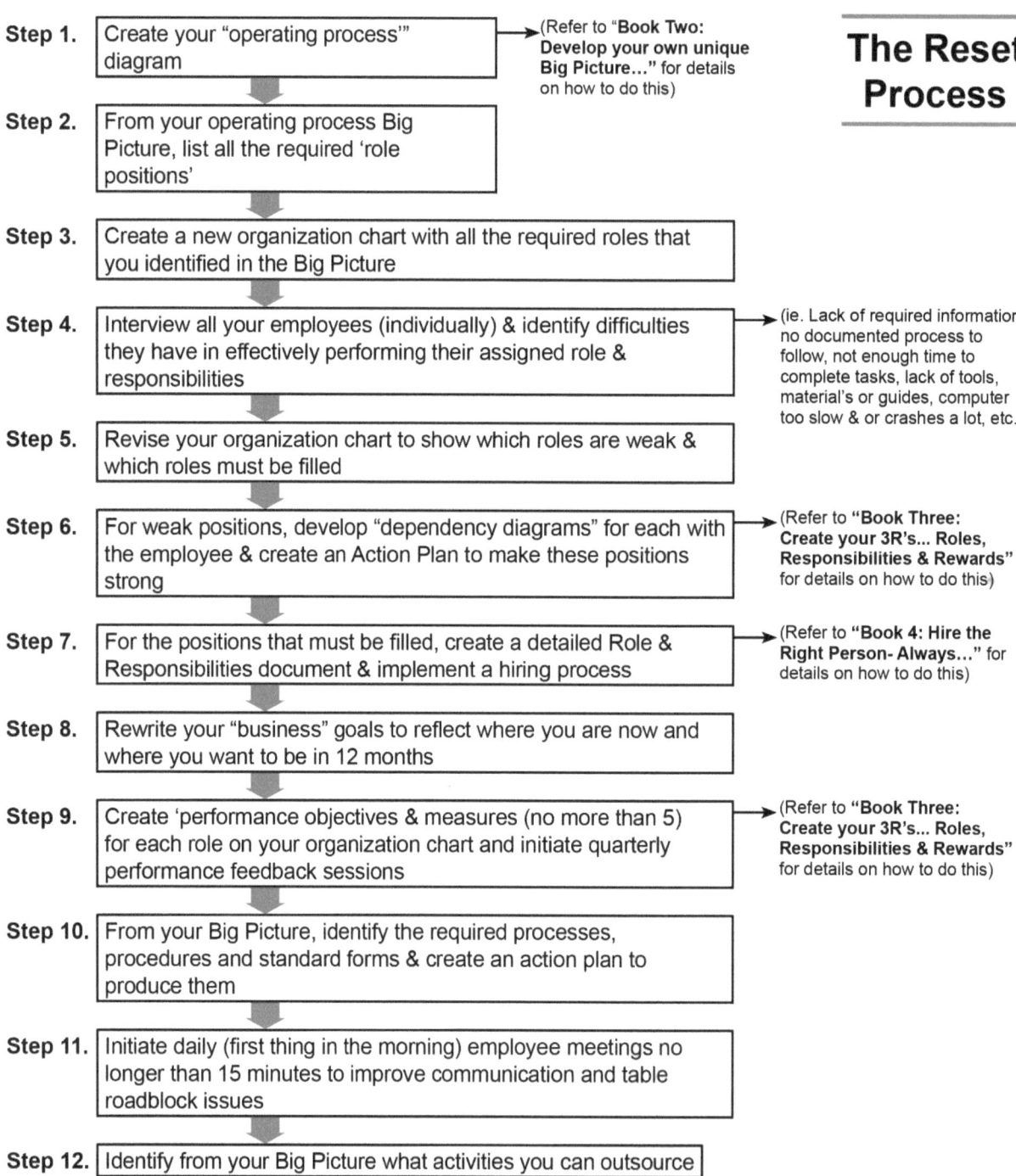

Step 1. Create your "operating process'" diagram
→ (Refer to "**Book Two: Develop your own unique Big Picture...**" for details on how to do this)

The Reset Process

Step 2. From your operating process Big Picture, list all the required 'role positions'

Step 3. Create a new organization chart with all the required roles that you identified in the Big Picture

Step 4. Interview all your employees (individually) & identify difficulties they have in effectively performing their assigned role & responsibilities
→ (ie. Lack of required information, no documented process to follow, not enough time to complete tasks, lack of tools, material's or guides, computer too slow & or crashes a lot, etc.)

Step 5. Revise your organization chart to show which roles are weak & which roles must be filled

Step 6. For weak positions, develop "dependency diagrams" for each with the employee & create an Action Plan to make these positions strong
→ (Refer to "**Book Three: Create your 3R's... Roles, Responsibilities & Rewards**" for details on how to do this)

Step 7. For the positions that must be filled, create a detailed Role & Responsibilities document & implement a hiring process
→ (Refer to "**Book 4: Hire the Right Person- Always...**" for details on how to do this)

Step 8. Rewrite your "business" goals to reflect where you are now and where you want to be in 12 months

Step 9. Create 'performance objectives & measures (no more than 5) for each role on your organization chart and initiate quarterly performance feedback sessions
→ (Refer to "**Book Three: Create your 3R's... Roles, Responsibilities & Rewards**" for details on how to do this)

Step 10. From your Big Picture, identify the required processes, procedures and standard forms & create an action plan to produce them

Step 11. Initiate daily (first thing in the morning) employee meetings no longer than 15 minutes to improve communication and table roadblock issues

Step 12. Identify from your Big Picture what activities you can outsource

Step One.   **Create your "Operating Process"**

You are going to 'draw' a picture of Your Business. Don't worry; you don't have to be a Picasso or Van Gogh. Simply use line drawings on a large blank piece of paper to show what happens in Your Business. A customer walks in the door, they talk to sales, sales writes up the request, the customer approves – then what happens? Where does the order go? Is there another approval process?

This diagram will give you an idea of what it should look like.

Start

Keep in mind that you will have to follow this process all the way through your company – to the point where your product or service is being shipped out the door.

Now you've got the beginnings of a 'flow' diagram for Your Business. Next add in where specific procedures and processes have to be applied in Your Business.

The following diagram will give you an idea.

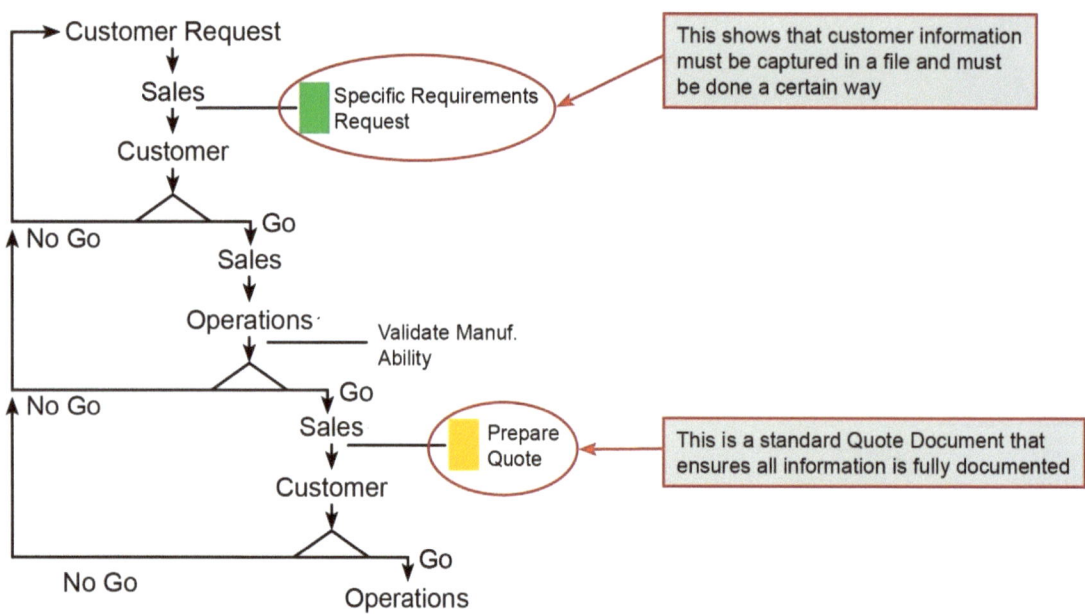

Again, keep in mind that you will follow the same process all the way through Your Business. Make sure you map in all the processes and procedures to where your product or service is being shipped out. (You'll find an example of a complete "Big Picture" at the end of the chapter).

You have created a simple version of Your Business "Big Picture".*

Your "Big Picture" is a great tool to communicate:

- How your business operates.

- What procedures and processes are required and where in your Big Picture they apply.

- What 'role positions' are required to run your business.

- How to promote your business operations to potential customers.

Now that you've got a good visual representation of Your Business, let's move on to Step Two and find out what roles you require to run Your Business effectively.

*You'll find detailed information in ***'Book Two – Develop Your Own Unique Big Picture…'.**

Step Two.   From your operating process "Big Picture" list your required 'role' positions.

Take a look at your flow process and list ALL the roles that you need to perform the tasks in Your Business. You'll likely have to modify your list so it reflects any unique processes that occur in Your Business.

Your list might include these roles:

- Sales

- Solution Design

- Administration

- Operations

- Production

- Assembly

- Inventory

- Building and packing

- Shipping/delivery

Now you have to figure out the volume, or how much work is required for EACH position. You need to do this for your present and predicted requirements. But now you know how many positions are needed for each task. This is the number of employees you need to efficiently run Your Business.

Here are a couple of examples of what your list of tasks might look like:

- **Operations.** Your predictions for growth indicate that you'll require a supervisor to run your production operation. Your supervisor will ensure that all safety and quality procedures and processes are followed. **Your Business needs one full-time Supervisor.**

- **Inventory.** You will need a very cost effective inventory at all times. Given your existing and predicted growth, your business must have the required supplies available at all times and at the best price. A delay would impact on your high standard of service. **Your Business needs one dedicated person to setup and manage your inventory.**

You get the idea. Now make notes on the work required for each position you identified. It might take a bit of time but you'll know exactly how many employees you need and where. When you're ready, move onto Step Three.

Step Three.   Create your new organization chart with all the new roles identified.

You'll now know (from Step 2) the number of full-time employees you need for your "Big Picture" to function effectively. Let's say you need 12 people to run Your Business.

So if you only have six employees trying to meet your current customer's demands, no wonder employee stress levels are up and everyone, you included is working long hours.

You now have two choices.

You either:

- Hire new employees to fill the required positions.

- Cut back on Your Business which means you must drop your new product line and/or downsize.

Either choice is a good one but you must make a decision.

HOWEVER

If you want to keep growing your business, you need to create a New Organization Chart.

The Required New Organization

Your New Organization Chart shows you the roles you need to effectively run Your Business. In Step Four you'll need to assess what you have by interviewing each individual employee.

Congratulations!

You've been doing a lot of work at fixing Your Business. Steps One, Two and Three are pretty visual, but sometimes that helps people to see where some of the issues exist. By kind of 'mind mapping' Your Business you get a different perspective and where you thought something was being done, maybe it wasn't. Step Four will really give you some insight into how your employees are feeling and some of the issues they're facing.

CHECKLIST:

Review Step One and make sure you included all the jobs/positions in your diagram. Also make sure you covered off ALL of your processes and procedures. Make a few notes below of any reminders you may need.

_____

_____

_____

_____

_____

Did you include all tasks for the roles your employees perform? Do a quick review.

Assuming you decided to keep growing Your Business, you've created a New Organization Chart. This should be reflective of your own unique business. You can make it as simple as you like but make sure you include all the roles needed to help you grow. Make notes below of any slight changes you might want to consider.

_____

_____

_____

_____

_____

_____

_____

Step Four. **Individually interview every employee and find out difficulties of assigned job and responsibilities.**

You're likely thinking, "What? Why?" You hired them all. Your Business is small. You know them all.

BUT

You need to interview each one of your employees 'in confidence' because:

- Your Business has changed since they started working for you.

- The work load has increased putting more pressure on all of you.

- Your Business's dynamics have changed.

Not only that, you've now got a New Organization Chart to help you reset Your Business.

You need to communicate to your employees exactly why you are conducting these interviews. You may be surprised how enthusiastically they welcome the opportunity to talk to you. Your employees, like you, are working hard, are stressed and want Your Business fixed too.

These are some basic questions to ask, you might want to add a few more:

- Can you get the necessary supplies you need to get your job done on time? If not, why not and be very specific.

- Does the equipment you use to do your job work well and efficiently all the time? If not what equipment isn't working and what equipment do you feel is missing?

- Do you feel safe in your work environment? If not, why not? Be specific.

- Did you receive adequate training to perform your assigned role to the best of your ability?

- Do you have all the information you need to do a great job? If not, why not? Be specific.

- Do you have enough time in the work day to get your assigned tasks completed? If not, why not? Be specific.

Now create a spreadsheet.

Column One will be the Subject - Equipment Function, Inventory Supplies, Safety, Training, Information, Time.

Column Two will be Issues - 'computer crashes 2 times a day', 'there is no safety training' or 'I'm working overtime and not getting the job done'.

Column Three will be Action Required – for the computer problem have them serviced regularly, bring in a safety expert to assess your needs, analyze your New Organization Chart and hire new employees.

Once you've completed your employee interviews, document the information in a spreadsheet. Use the six questions as subjects. Summarize what needs to be done.

Interview for Reset

Subject	Issue	Action Required
Equipment Function	• Computer #3 crashes 2 times a day • Inventory computer is way to slow • Do not have adequate s/w for the required design solution functions	Get an outsourced contract to service all our computers regularly Contact design s/w supplier, bring them in and upgrade if required
Inventory Supplies	• There never is enough file folders when you need them • Fasteners are quite often the wrong one's and/or there are never enough	Introducing a computer driven spreadsheet to be managed by the inventory role and, include status in bi-weekly reporting
Safety	• There is no safety training, so we do the best we can • There is only one fire extinguisher	Bring in local safety expert to assess your total Health & Safety need, produce a training module and implement
Training	• I had no orientation training when I started • I have not been trained on the new design s/w tools	Create a business orientation presentation and give to all employees at a general meeting. Send design employees on the design tool training course… try to have it done in house
Information	• I always have to go after the information I need and that wastes a lot of time • We need better handout information about our business	Initiate every morning, 15 minute meetings at 8 am with all employees to table roadblocking issues and give specific instructions for the day. Have a folder or fact sheet about your business.
Time	• I used to have no problem getting my work done each day. I am now working a lot of overtime and I still don't get my work done.	Analyze the proposed new organization and finalize the number of new employees that are required to meet your customer demand.

Step Five. **Revise your organization chart to show weak roles and new ones to be filled.**

Now you can identify any weak positions on your New Organization Chart. Your employee interviews will also have revealed which employees are having trouble. You'll also be able to identify which positions need to be filled as well as areas of duplication that can be eliminated or streamlined.

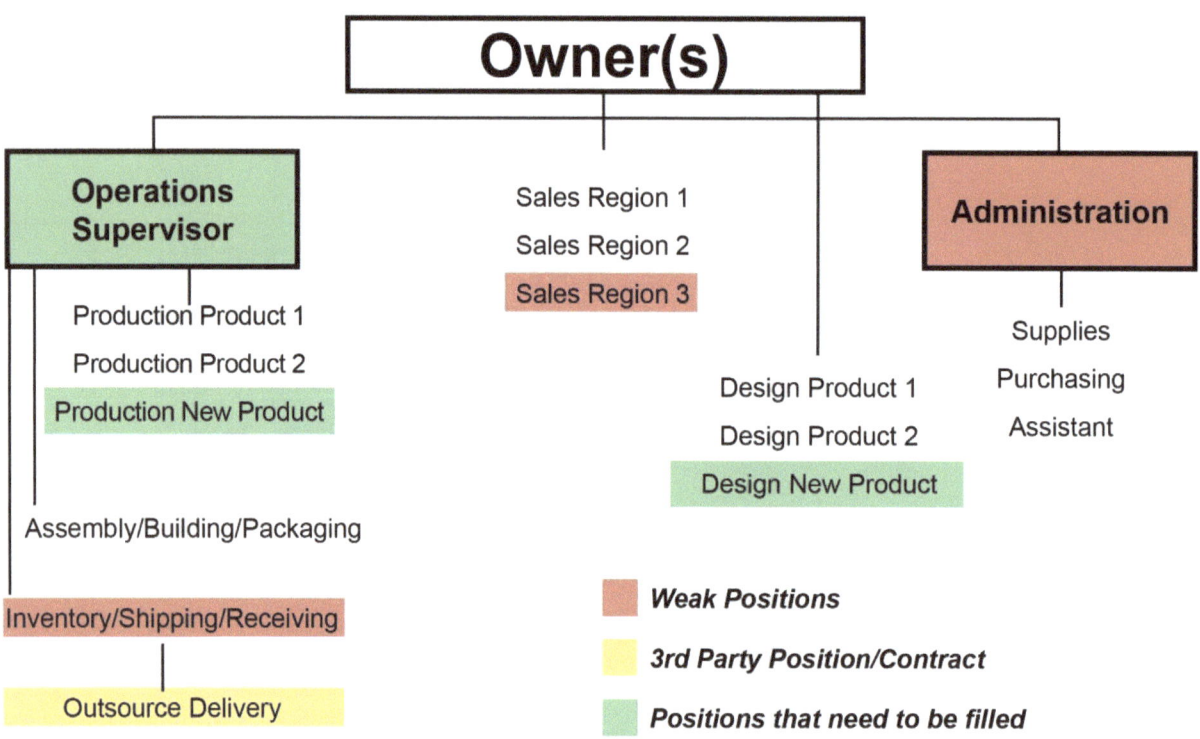

You've discovered by going through this process the reasons you've been stressed, your employees have been stressed and the reasons you've had issues in your operation – including customer complaints.

These are the reasons it feels like "the wheels are falling off Your Business":

- You have three (3) positions that are currently filled, but weak. (Step 6 will discuss what to do). Weak positions translate to inefficiencies and errors that reflect on Your Business.

- You need three (3) positions filled immediately so Your Business can meet the current demand. (Step 7 will discuss what to do). Your production and design employees were trying to handle the additional workload. They expressed these issues and told about the problems they were having in their "Interview for Reset".

- You discovered the high cost of getting your products to your customers. You had to license, maintain and insure your vehicles to do this. Your handling/shipping/inventory and receiving employee was on the road 35% of the time. Their other work suffered. Among other things you discovered that outsourcing deliveries to an established shipping company was one third the cost. You could free up your resource by 30% to cover inventory and allot time to manage the shipping and receiving function.

You now have to fix your weak positions and hire additional employees.

Step Six.   **Develop 'dependency diagrams' for weak roles and an Action Plan to strengthen these positions.**

IMPORTANT

DO NOT assume you know why your employee is not doing a good job. Using your subjective assessment is the kiss of death in business. In my experience, many times a good employee was fired for reasons that were completely out of their control.

DO sit down with your employee and create a "dependency map". Identify who depends on them and who they depend on to get their job done. By doing this you'll remove any subjective judgement and more accurately identify why things aren't going as well as they should.

NOW

Look at the three roles that are weak.

Your three weak roles "dependency maps" might look like this:

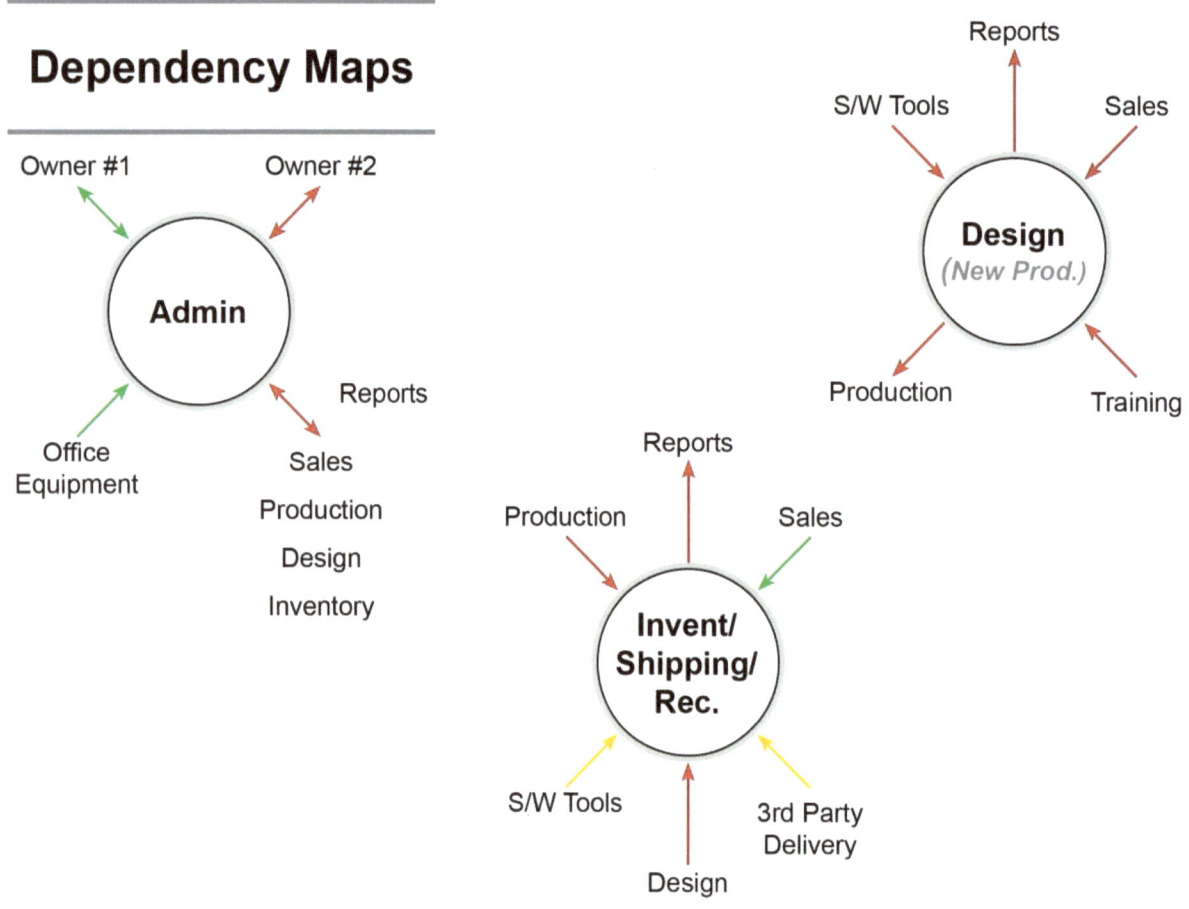

Green arrows indicate that the dependencies are strong. No issues here.

Yellow arrows indicate a potential issue. Your inventory/shipping receiving employee expressed concern with 3rd party delivery and software issues. If Your Business is going to grow, this could be a problem but these should be easy fixes.

Red arrows indicate a real problem. They show your lack of ability to deliver along with Your Business growth.

Your Business and your employees are struggling in three roles, Administration, Design and Inventory, Shipping & Receiving.

Can you spot the problems in the dependency map example?

Here are a few of examples:

The Administration Role:

- Owner #2 has performance issues. Owner #2 is difficult to reach and doesn't respond quickly. Owner #2 is out of the office a good part of each day handling sales. Your Business needs to hire additional sales staff to fix the problem.

- Your administrator consistently issues reports late to the business owners. However, the information for the reports has to be provided by sales, production, design and inventory. The increased workload in these positions has delayed getting the information to the administrator which causes the delay in reports to the owners.

Design Role.

- Every dependency for this role is weak. Your first reaction may be to fire the designers. However, you can see that your designers are at the mercy of just about everyone and everything.

- Sales can barely keep up with selling. They are consistently late providing design with the customer needs. Your designers then feel huge pressure to get the design documents into production.

- Design is overloaded with designing so report information is delayed getting to administration.

Inventory, Shipping & Receiving.

- Information arriving late from design impacts on the ability to order required materials on time.

- Production is late in building and assembling due to lack of materials. This causes shipping to be late getting the product to the 3rd party delivery.

- The backlog of work inventory delays any report information to Administration.

Your Business's increased workload and lack of tools to handle more information is significantly impacting your employee's ability to get their work done and do it correctly.

Your fixes are simple. Your improvements will be huge.

You now need to hire three people for the positions you identified in your organization chart.

Congratulations!

You're probably finding out a few things you didn't realize about Your Business. Steps Four, Five and Six really delve into how employees and their job responsibilities work. You now should have further insight – especially from the information you gathered in Step Four – about how your employees are feeling and the issues they're facing. Do a review below of what you've learned. Then move onto the next three steps for insight into hiring, business goals and performance objectives.

CHECKLIST:

Review the spreadsheet you created. This should provide you with some of the issues your employees are facing.

Make notes below about what you discovered about the weak roles in your business. Add a few more details if needed.

_____
_____
_____
_____
_____
_____
_____

Review your Dependency Map. Jot down below how you will start to put together your Action Plan.

_____
_____
_____
_____
_____
_____
_____

Step Seven. **For new positions create a list of Roles and Responsibilities and implement a hiring process.**

Your Business not only needs to hire people, Your Business has to hire the right people. You have to accurately and completely identify the role(s) you want to fill.

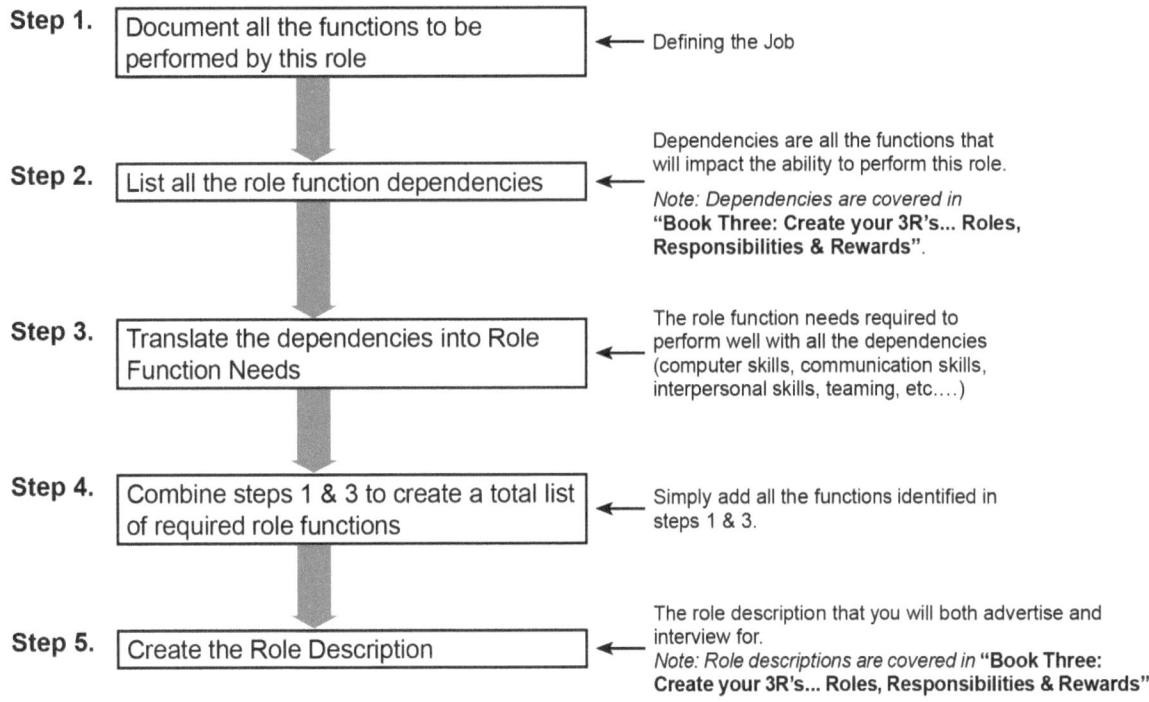

The chart above is from *'Book Four – Hire the Right Person - Always…'*.

REMEMBER

Hiring of the wrong person can have a huge and costly impact on Your Business.

Step Eight.   Rewrite Your Businesses goals to reflect where you are now, where you want to be in a year.

Here's a quick review of the tools you now have available:

- You have a map of how Your Business works – The Big Picture.

- You know where the weak roles are.

- You know the roles that have to be filled.

- You have an Action Plan so day to day performance is strengthened.

Now, revisit your original business goals, the ones you set when you started Your Business.

You need to do this because:

- Your output had increased 150% to meet customer demand over the last year or two.

- Your original sales targets have been exceeded by close to 200%.

- Your floor space is no longer adequate.

- You have to open a new location to serve new customers.

- You've decided to diversify.

NONE OF THIS WAS IN YOUR ORIGINAL GOAL DESCRIPTION.

Your Business has far exceeded what you predicted. By doing a RESET Your Business can grow and embrace the future potential.

You now have more experience in running Your Business. You know your market and your opportunities.

Your Business RESET will also align your employees to your new objectives.*

* 'Book Three – Create your 3R's…Roles, Responsibilities & Rewards', explains how to set performance objectives for your employees so they align with your business goals and ensure success if met.

Step Nine. **Create up to Five Performance Objectives and Measures for each role on your organization chart.**

Your Objectives and Measures:

- No more than four or five for each employee.

- Keep it simple so employees can do their own assessments on an ongoing basis. .

Objectives & Measures ensure the following:

- Performance is measured with specific measures rather than subjective ones.

- Concise measures help your employees determine how well they are performing in their roles.

- Your Business goals will be met, possibly exceeded because each of your employees' objectives and measures are a subset of Your Business's goals.

For example:

Does Your Business have "Sales Targets"? Then your goal may be to achieve 2.5 million in sales in region 2. Your sales region 2 employees' **objective** says: "*must effectively carry out the sales responsibility for region 2 without receiving any customer complaints*". Your employee's **measure** might say: "*has to achieve sales of 2.5 million and a customer satisfaction rating of 7.5/10*". Your employee knows that by achieving the sales target, they've achieved their objective.

High customer satisfaction ratings mean your business will grow in that region.

Your customers will be loyal to Your Business.

Remember:

When your employees achieve, Your Business achieves. It's as simple as that.

MAKE SURE YOU'VE STARTED QUARTERLY FEEDBACK SESSIONS.

(This will be covered in detail in
'Book Three – Create your 3R's – Roles, Responsibilities, Rewards').

Step Ten deals with identifying all the forms, procedures and processes you need to run Your Business. This is all part of completing your "Big Picture".

Congratulations!

Whew! That was a lot of work. But now you know not only how to hire the right person, but you've got a great job description that you can use for your advertisements and for the job interview process. You've also got an up to date set of Business Goals and my guess is your employees and probably you too are happier working now that you have Objectives and Measures in place. Everyone is now working from the 'same page', so to speak. You'll also find the quarterly feedback sessions will really improve your employees' performance.

Only three more steps to completing Your Business Reset. Do a quick review below and move onto Step Ten.

Review the new Role Descriptions you created. You should always be fine-tuning your descriptions. Make notes below on things you might want to add.

_____

_____

_____

_____

_____

Review Your Business Goals and make sure you have covered all the changes to Your Business. Jot down any fine-tuning you want to do below.

_____

_____

_____

_____

_____

How has morale improved with Objectives and Measures in place? What insights are you getting from the feedback sessions?

_____

_____

_____

_____

_____

Step Ten.   **Use your Big Picture to identify processes, procedures and forms now required to run Your Business. Follow an action plan to get them done.**

Don't overdo the documents!

Only implement what you need. Keep your documents simple. You want your employees focused on doing their job not on filling out documentation and forms.

These definitions can help you run Your Business:

Procedures. They provide a guide for the critical operations of a business. These are examples of procedures for Your Business:

- Sales

- Service Delivery

- Quality

- Safety

- Purchasing

- Filing

Processes. A process is contained within a procedure. A process describes the step-by-step method used to ensure repeatability and consistency all the time, no matter who is doing the job.

Forms. A form(s) is contained in each process. Forms ensure that when information is captured, it's always captured in the same format all the time, no matter who is doing the job.

Procedures, Processes and Forms ensure:

- When something goes wrong, you can easily find out where, and how to fix it.

- Continuous improvement.

- Good business growth.

Now, go back to your "Big Picture" and identify what Procedures, Processes and Forms Your Business needs.

Helpful Hint

Colour-code your Procedures, Processes and Forms – it will make them easier to identify on your Big Picture. Procedures – green, Processes – yellow, Forms – pink. You get the idea.

For example Your Business might need:

An Administration Procedure:

- A filing procedure so all required customer and job information is kept in order, is complete at all times and readily retrievable.

Forms:

- A "Customer Request" form that contains all the required information to fully process a job request. This form is important, especially if the customer changes their mind or asks for changes to the original order.

- A "Customer Satisfaction" form – especially for sales to see if they are meeting customer needs. This is crucial data for planning business growth and assessing customer needs.

An Operations Process or Processes:

- The specific fabrication and assembly processes that must be followed. This ensures that customer requests are met.

- Quality processes to ensure a consistently high product standard.

- Safety processes so you have the minimum number of accidents and to reduce insurance costs.

- You also require a packaging process for shipping the finished product and to ensure the product is protected during shipping and handling.

Responsibilities:

Your "Big Picture" needs Two Procedures, Five Processes - both basic and simple, and Two Forms that are pretty standard. That's it.

Your procedures should be no more than five to ten pages each. Your processes should be a single page with a step-by-step flow chart.

Your administrative employee should develop and 'own' the administration procedures as well as any related forms.

Your operations employee should develop and 'own' the operations procedure as well as the fabrications/assembly, quality, safety and packaging processes.

Your Business will be reflected in these documents, so you must have final approval of the original documents and you have to approve any changes requested.

Your Procedure, Process and Form documents should be reviewed and updated as required and as Your Business grows.

You can customize what Your Business needs.

You decide what Procedures, Processes and Forms Your Business might need.

You get final approval and you have to approve any changes requested.

REMEMBER

As Your Business grows make sure you review and update your Procedure, Process and Forms documents.

Step Eleven. **Hold daily morning meetings of 15 minutes to improve communication and discover potential roadblock issues.**

Lack of Information.

My guess is that lack of information is one of the weaknesses your employees commented on in the interviews you did. More than likely, everyone gets so wrapped up in their jobs they forget to communicate with each other. But you and your employees need to know what is going on with the business and this should be on a daily basis.

But we do have meetings!

You likely hold a regular monthly meeting that lasts half a day. That's information overload. Your employees just want to get back to work.

Instead hold a 15 minute meeting the first thing every morning and:

- Your 15 minute meeting will become a habit.

- It also means you don't have to try and accommodate everyone's schedules.

- Your meeting happens at the same place at the same time every morning.

- Your meeting is short and to the point. Downtime is at a minimum.

- Your employees are more focused because they haven't started work yet.

- You can address roadblocks and agree on an action plan.

- You can make business announcements that your employees should know about.

- Your daily morning meeting can nip rumours in the bud. Instead they are discussed and resolved.

- You get to be on top of Your Business's tempo. That helps you to know how to manage your employees and Your Business.

Step Twelve. Identify what can be outsourced from your Big Picture.

Your Business has grown. You used to be able to visit your third party outsourcing partners.

Realize that someone in Your Business has to manage any outsourcing.

Your outsourcing might include these areas:

- Accounting

- Specialized jobs that require specific skills such as, logo development, very tight tolerances, assembling documents, graphics and IT.

- Shipping/Delivery

- Finishing that requires a special setup such as plating and printing

- Research

Outsourcing must be managed by one of the role positions in Your Business.

For example:

- Your design employee can deal with outsourced design.

- Inventory can handle Shipping/Delivery.

- Your production employee can handle outsourced finishing.

You get the idea.

HOWEVER:

As the business owner you must deal with all the accounting and finances. In a small business those roles stay with the owners, always.

Congratulations!

You made it through the Twelve Steps. That was a lot of work. But the wheels are back on the bus, so to speak. You've got some good processes, procedures and forms in place to keep things on track. Those 15 minute morning meetings are going to help improve communication and you can breathe a sigh of relief that some of the trickier or too time consuming aspects of your production can be outsourced to reliable third parties. Fill in the checklists below with anything you want to remember for later. You're well on your way to a Business Reset that will keep Your Business running smoothly.

What procedures, processes and forms are you going to add?

List some areas of discussion that should be part of your 15 minute morning meeting.

_____
_____
_____
_____
_____

What parts of your production are you now thinking of outsourcing? How will you benefit?

_____
_____
_____
_____
_____

CHAPTER FIVE

An Introduction to a "Big Picture"

In the next book you'll find out how Your Big Picture is going to help you identify all the essential procedures that make Your Business successful and highlight the areas where the 'wheels might be falling off'. When you document ALL the steps you go through to get your product to your customer, your Big Picture will highlight the area where problems and issues might arise. This introduction will lay out some basic steps and actions for you.

Here are some examples:

QUALITY CONTROL

- You need a procedure to ensure your high quality every time.

- You need to identify where mistakes in quality can happen.

If your service/product is not up to expectations Your Business could lose contracts.

MAINTENANCE PROCEDURES

- Your Big Picture will remind you when to do your maintenance.

- You can pinpoint production and delivery issues.

If you can't produce, you can't deliver.

FILING SYSTEM

- You need a system where material is easy to find and up-to-date.

- Your billing system must be accurate and timely.

If you're not billing on time, or incorrectly you won't get paid.

SERVICE/PRODUCT INSPECTION PROCEDURE

- Your service/product must meet customer expectations.

- You can pinpoint how to prevent loss of efficiency in your process.

If your service/product is incomplete or doesn't meet your standards, you lose customers.

PACKAGING/DELIVERING YOUR SERVICE/PRODUCT

- Your procedure must ensure consistency in packaging.

- Your procedure must ensure there is no damage during handling and delivery.

  If it has to be replaced it means lost revenue and/or a damaged reputation.

MORE ESSENTIAL 'BIG PICTURE' BENEFITS:

- Clearly shows value and relationship of your employees.

- Shows responsibility, accountability and role dependencies.

- Lays out all your required procedures and processes for employees.

- Identifies where your problems occur.

- Provides a visual insight so you can create a permanent fix.

ALSO

Your Big Picture is **an excellent marketing tool**. It shows existing and potential customers how Your Business is predictable, organized and delivers quality services/products.

Your Big Picture is **an excellent Orientation Presentation** for both your existing and new employees.

Your Big Picture is your visual map of how Your Business works.

It really is a step-by-step view of how your customer ends up with your final service/product. Your Big Picture can show you:

- Why sales are down.

- Where the real issues are in your business process.

- Who is responsible for certain jobs.

- What procedures or processes aren't working.

- How you can get your service/product to your customer on time.

You may have already come up with 'symbols' that represent the flow of Your Businesses Big Picture. Or you can use 'standard symbols' like you'd find in a program like Visio Microsoft. I've used the symbols below for many Big Pictures and find them useful. Make sure you denote what they mean so everyone can follow your diagram.

SYMBOLS FOR YOUR BIG PICTURE:

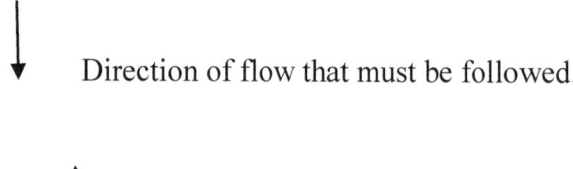 Direction of flow that must be followed.

This is a decision point in your process.

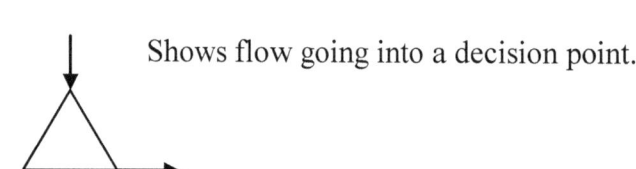 Shows flow going into a decision point.

This shows that the decision is 'to proceed' in the flow. In other words, the customer has approved the quote, the materials/capacity to do the job are in stock/available etc...

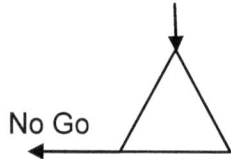

This indicates that the decision is 'not to proceed' with the flow. For example, the customer has not accepted the quote or wants changes, or a new quote. Or maybe there isn't enough material or capacity to do the job. Note that the flow will show an arrow going back to the beginning or back to a specific stage.

This represents a specific form, process or procedure at that stage that has to be filled in and/or followed.

Again, I found these easy to work with and the arrows are pretty self-evident so just about anyone can understand how your Big Picture is laid out. Use whatever works for you.

Congratulations!

Are you starting to see just why having your Big Picture is so essential? It really does lay out Your Business in black and white (well with some colours for your Procedures, Processes and Forms!) and it's easy for not just you to follow, but your employees as well. You can visually 'see' where some of your problems and issues arise. My guess is you're also realizing just which procedures are essential. Only two chapters left! Keep going!

CHAPTER CHECKLIST:

What "essential procedures" did you identify that you really need to keep Your Business running smoothly?

_____

_____

_____

_____

_____

Did you find any surprises in how Your Business was running? What was working and what areas need to be changed? Note them below.

_____

_____

_____

_____

_____

What symbols do you use? Make sure they're consistent throughout your Big Picture and your employees understand their meaning. Make any notes below.

_____

_____

_____

CHAPTER SIX

Review Your Business Reset

Really. I mean it. Now that you know the 'why', I want you to go back and review the 'how'. Go through each one of the twelve steps in Chapter Four. It will help cement for you what you've found out about your business, reinforce the new procedures you have in place and keep you focused on moving forward.

You now have:

- A "Big Picture" diagram that visually represents how your business operates.

- A list of roles and positions that are needed to keep your business functioning.

- A new organization chart for your business with any new roles identified.

- An understanding of the issues and problems that your employees face on a day-to-day basis.

- An awareness of where the weak roles exist in your business and which ones need to be filled.

- An action plan that shows you how to strengthen dependencies in weak areas.

- A hiring process with a list of Roles and Responsibilities required when filling those positions.

- A set of goals for your business for the next year.

- A list of objectives and measures for your business.

- An action plan for creating the procedures, processes and forms that are required to make your business run smoothly.

- A morning motivation meeting to discuss issues and boost morale.

- A realization of what can be outsourced to better your production.

The Bottom Line?

Your Business is efficient. Your employees are satisfied. You're making money.

Congratulations!

Did you do it? A complete review? The more you understand the 'how', the more ingrained it will become to how you operate Your Business. You'll know the minute that something isn't working quite right and it feels like the wheels are loose. You'll be able to quickly go through your reset and pinpoint the problem or issue. Not only that, now that you know how to 'reset' Your Business, the minute that you expand or grow Your Business you can quickly plug in the changes you have to make to keep "the wheels from falling off".

If you have any questions just ask. I'm only a phone call or an email away. And remember, no question is too trivial; sometimes the smallest thing can create an enormous stumbling block.

CHAPTER CHECKLIST:

Make any notes on your review below – it will ensure that you remember.

_____

_____

_____

_____

_____

_____

_____

_____

_____

CHAPTER SEVEN

The Next Steps For Your Business Success

You're now ready to move onto Book Two. I'm going to walk you through the creation of Your Businesses own Big Picture. I know I touched on the basics in Chapter Five of this book. Book Two contains a completed and fairly complex Big Picture example. Keep in mind the benefits mentioned in this book – quality control, procedures for filing, service and delivery. Big Picture benefits also include these essentials:

- Clearly shows value and relationship of your employees.

- Shows responsibility, accountability and role dependencies.

- Lays out all your required procedures and processes for employees.

- Identifies where your problems occur.

- Provides a visual insight so you can create a permanent fix.

Keep this in mind as you start *'Book Two – Develop Your Own Unique Big Picture…'* it is going to force you to think about and document all of the steps that are necessary to get your product to your customer.

Your Big Picture is going to be a visual map of how Your Business works.

Congratulations!

If you're reading this then you've gone through the review and you're really serious about moving on to *'Book Two – Develop Your Own Unique Big Picture…'*. Your Business will benefit from what you're going to learn. *'Book Three – Create your 3R's…Roles, Responsibilities & Rewards'* will deal with Roles, Responsibilities and Rewards and make sure you follow up with the bonus material. It'll ensure that you get the best person for the job – all the time. Your Business wheels are going to be firmly on and Your Business should be humming along nicely. Good work!

If you have any questions just ask. I'm only a phone call or an email away. And remember, no question is too trivial; sometimes the smallest thing can create an enormous stumbling block.

Peter Maheux – Your Business Reset Expert.

Questions? Visit **www.meetme.so/businessreset** and schedule your personal call!

BOOK TWO - YOUR NEXT STEP

Business Reset 2.0 – How to Fix Your Business when the Wheels Fall Off – Develop Your Own Unique Big Picture

Visit www.BusinessReset.com for full stories and testimonials from a number of companies I've helped 'reset'. You may find issues and problems you can easily relate to for Your Business!

As promised – on the following page is a diagram for a fairly complex "Big Picture".

DO NOT BE AFRAID!

How to create your own "Big Picture" is outlined in the next book. You'll be able to create your own detailed "Big Picture". Even if you're a 'one-man-band' a detailed 'picture' of how your business operates will keep you on top of how your business runs and you'll have a more balanced lifestyle.

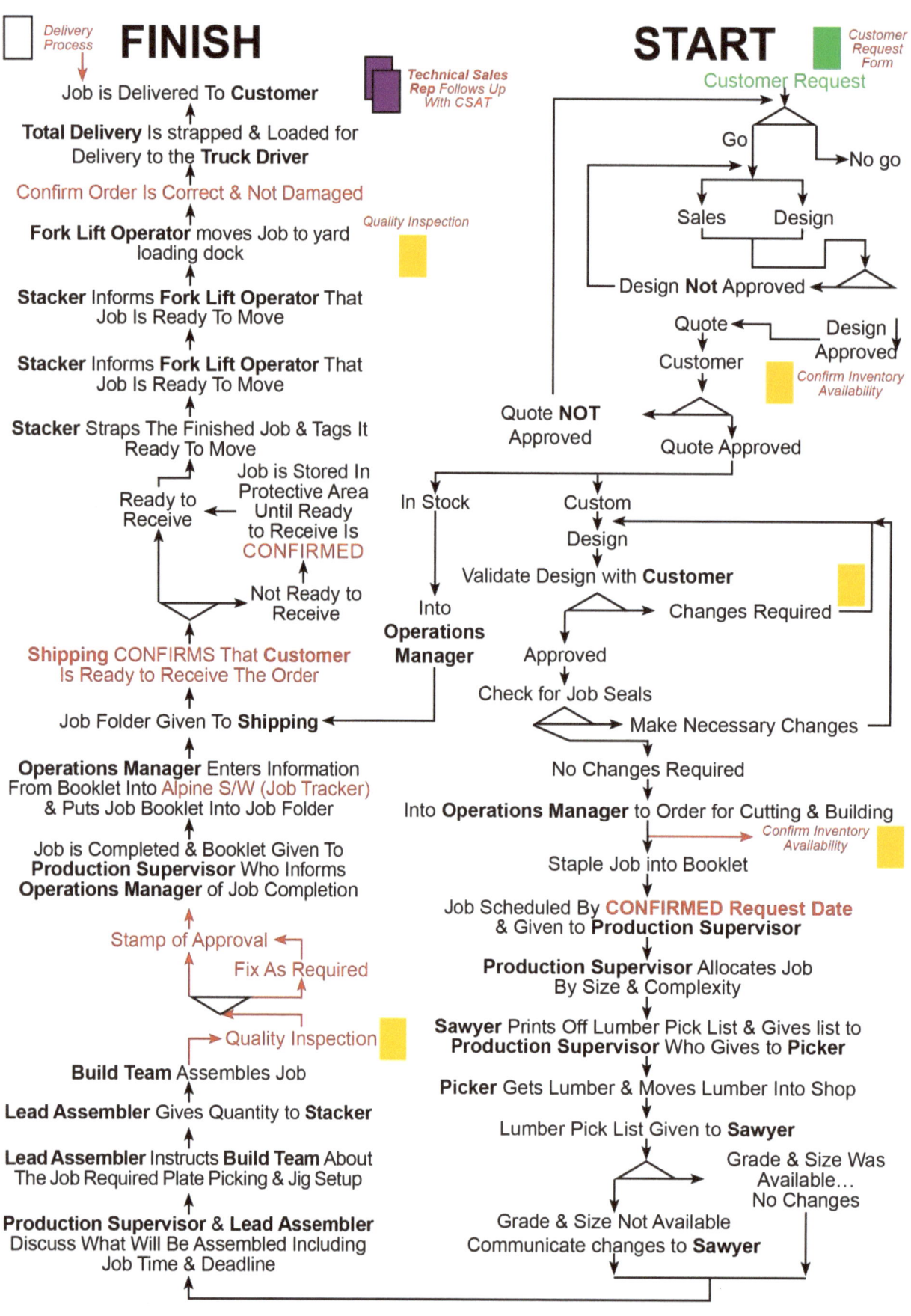

FINISH

Job is Delivered To **Customer**

Total Delivery Is strapped & Loaded for Delivery to the **Truck Driver**

Confirm Order Is Correct & Not Damaged

Fork Lift Operator moves Job to yard loading dock

Stacker Informs **Fork Lift Operator** That Job Is Ready To Move

Stacker Informs **Fork Lift Operator** That Job Is Ready To Move

Stacker Straps The Finished Job & Tags It Ready To Move

Ready to Receive

Job is Stored In Protective Area Until Ready to Receive Is CONFIRMED

Not Ready to Receive

Shipping CONFIRMS That **Customer** Is Ready to Receive The Order

Job Folder Given To **Shipping**

Operations Manager Enters Information From Booklet Into Alpine S/W (Job Tracker) & Puts Job Booklet Into Job Folder

Job is Completed & Booklet Given To **Production Supervisor** Who Informs **Operations Manager** of Job Completion

Stamp of Approval

Fix As Required

Quality Inspection

Build Team Assembles Job

Lead Assembler Gives Quantity to **Stacker**

Lead Assembler Instructs **Build Team** About The Job Required Plate Picking & Jig Setup

Production Supervisor & **Lead Assembler** Discuss What Will Be Assembled Including Job Time & Deadline

Delivery Process

Technical Sales Rep Follows Up With CSAT

Quality Inspection

START

Customer Request

Customer Request Form

Go

No go

Sales

Design

Design **Not** Approved

Quote

Customer

Design Approved

Confirm Inventory Availability

Quote **NOT** Approved

Quote Approved

In Stock

Custom

Design

Validate Design with **Customer**

Changes Required

Into **Operations Manager**

Approved

Check for Job Seals

Make Necessary Changes

No Changes Required

Into **Operations Manager** to Order for Cutting & Building

Confirm Inventory Availability

Staple Job into Booklet

Job Scheduled By CONFIRMED Request Date & Given to **Production Supervisor**

Production Supervisor Allocates Job By Size & Complexity

Sawyer Prints Off Lumber Pick List & Gives list to **Production Supervisor** Who Gives to **Picker**

Picker Gets Lumber & Moves Lumber Into Shop

Lumber Pick List Given to **Sawyer**

Grade & Size Was Available… No Changes

Grade & Size Not Available Communicate changes to **Sawyer**

46